Read-Aloud Plays
PIONEERS

by
Dallas Murphy

SCHOLASTIC
PROFESSIONAL BOOKS

New York • Toronto • London • Auckland • Sydney • Mexico City • New Delhi • Hong Kong

Cover design by Jaime Lucero

Interior design by Ellen Hassell for Boultinghouse & Boultinghouse, Inc.

Cover and interior illustrations by Mona Mark

ISBN 0-590-91811-7

Contents

Introduction

Who were the pioneers? Why did these Americans leave family, friends, and their familiar surroundings for a new and uncertain future? The five original plays in this book will help to deepen and broaden students' understanding of the pioneer experience.

The first play, *Time Travel,* sets the stage. Here students will travel back in time to learn about the Louisiana Purchase. In *Letters Home,* they gain an understanding of the difficulties, challenges, and excitement of traveling along the Oregon Trail. *The Shortcut* gives students insight into the tough decisions pioneers faced and introduces them to the mountain men. *The Cake Wreck* tells the story of pioneers in Florida. And finally, *A Visitor* presents Laura Ingalls Wilder as an 83-year-old woman looking back on her pioneer life and the changes she's seen since then.

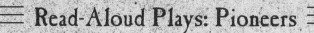

The Importance of Read-Aloud Plays

Read-aloud plays are a powerful classroom tool. Students often struggle to find connections between their own lives and the social studies topics they are studying. They often see the content as unrelated and unconnected to the stories in their own lives. The read-aloud plays in this book can provide opportunities for students to make these connections, to explore content in a way that is truly meaningful to middle-grade students. Taking on a role, even for a very short time, allows learners to become part of the story of our history, to become emotionally involved in it.

The read-aloud format gives more students a chance to participate in a classroom activity. For many students, the prospect of reading a few short lines at a time is far less intimidating than having to work through a block-like paragraph. Repetition of lines is another valuable feature of plays. Reading and rereading the same material is unappetizing drill work for most students. But it's different with plays. The players want to get it right. This is the best kind of learning.

Description of the Plays and Teaching Guide

This collection has been designed to enrich your existing curriculum. Since these plays can be read aloud as well as acted, incorporating them into your classroom will strengthen oral literacy and reading skills. Knowing that they can read the plays aloud may lessen some students' anxiety about performing. Those students who enjoy acting can personalize their roles with body movement. There are also suggested stage directions. You may want to reproduce the glossary on page 63, which explains various theater terms, for students.

Everyone should be encouraged to take on a role and participate in the cooperative effort of the group. Rotate roles so everyone has a chance to appear in a play. This can be a great way to spawn discussion. Girls may protest that they can't play male roles; boys may resist female roles. Although race and gender are often specific and important in the events described, they don't matter in the casting of the plays. In fact, playing characters very different from themselves may deepen students' insight into the times and events.

A teaching guide follows each play. The guide begins with a section called **The Story Behind the Play,** which gives historical background about the play and provides further context. The **Bibliography** suggests books students may enjoy reading. In the **Activities** section, there are ideas for cross-curricular activities that emphasize discussion, writing, research, and cooperative learning. Small groups or the entire class may participate in the discussion activities. Many writing activities center around individual writing, but students should be encouraged to share their work with their classmates. Also, small groups may want to collaborate on writing projects and create a book of their work. A small group may also tackle a research project; members may undertake different topics or avenues and then come together in the group to collate their information.

The teaching guide is exactly that—a guide. Feel free to use it as a starting point and expand any of the sections. Encourage students to create activities that correspond to their own interests. You may want to broaden the scope of this book by having students research and then write their own plays about other events that took place during America's pioneer days.

How to Present the Plays

Before students read through a play, make available books suggested in the bibliography—and any others that you particularly like. Share the historical background of the event to provide students with a context. Because the plays are tailored for a wide audience, students may find it helpful to cull a vocabulary list from the text.

Depending on the size of your class, you may want to assign two or three students to a part before you begin. In this way, students can switch into roles easily during a scene break. This will allow even more students to participate. At the end of each scene, take a break and ask a critical-thinking question. This will allow students to process what they've heard and clear some space for student questions.

After a first read-through of the play, you may want to assign the activities, especially the ones involving discussion, to get students talking about the event and the way it was portrayed. And, depending on how elaborate your productions get, some of the writing and research activities can have an impact on the script, sets, and costumes. You may find that students get more adventurous as they become comfortable with the structure of the plays and activities. Your class may go from simply reading the plays without any embellishments to putting on full-scale productions for schoolmates, families, and friends!

Again, the goal of these plays is to involve students not only with the past but also with the present. Students should feel that they can be any of the characters, regardless of their own backgrounds or the characters'. Some students may enjoy the role of the narrator. Others may blossom as they step into other people's lives. Some of the plays contain crowd scenes; these roles provide excellent opportunities for ad-libbing. The readers' theater format offers a non-threatening way to encourage student participation, and what better way to learn than by doing?

Time Travel

CAST

STAN CHAMPION, Reporter for the Time Travel Television Network

HOLLY HOLIDAY, Reporter for the Time Travel Television Network

DR. OSGOOD CONKLIN, Historical adviser for the Time Travel Television Network

TALLYRAND (1754–1838), Grand chamberlain of France

TALLYRAND'S SECRETARY

JAMES MONROE (1758–1831), United States diplomat; later fifth U.S. president

RED JACKET (1750?–1830), Iroquois Indian chief

THOMAS JEFFERSON (1743–1826), Third president of the United States

JOSEPH FOSTER, Pioneer in the Willamette Valley, Oregon Territory

MARTHA FOSTER, Joseph's wife

OWEN FOSTER, Joseph and Martha's son

EMILY FOSTER, Joseph and Martha's daughter

Read-Aloud Plays: Pioneers Scholastic Professional Books

Scene. Various places during the first half of the nineteenth century—Washington, D.C., in 1793 and in 1804; Paris, France, in 1803; the Williamette Valley in Oregon Territory in 1848.

(The people from the past are all sitting on chairs upstage. They "become" their character only when they stand up. While seated upstage, they are more like audience members.)

(STAN CHAMPION enters.)

STAN: Hello, everyone! I'm Stan Champion, and welcome to the Time Travel Television Network.

(The other characters applaud.)

Any study of history is a sort of time travel. We go backward in our minds to understand what life was like for those who came before us. But now, thanks to Virtual Vision, we can actually go back in time and meet our predecessors. Well, not *actually*. Virtually. Actually, it's a very complicated process, and I don't pretend to understand it. The engineers and technicians understand it. Some of them, anyway. The technology is in its infancy, like, say, the Internet in 1999. I can't be certain I'll land in the right place and time, but here goes—

(Some kind of special effect to indicate time travel—music, perhaps. The stage returns to normal. STAN is alone onstage.)

STAN: Okay, I think we made it. (He looks at his watch.) Yes. It's 1848, in the Willamette Valley, Oregon Territory. You can see why people worked so hard to get here. It's gorgeous, a long evergreen forest with plenty of water. In fact, it rains all winter, but farmers love that. The Foster claim is just down the hill. While I make my way down, I'll pass you over to Holly Holiday, who's waiting back in 1803. She'll show you how all this pioneering got started in the first place. Over to you, Holly.

(STAN exits stage left. HOLLY enters stage right. Meanwhile, TALLYRAND stands and brings his chair to the middle of the stage.)

HOLLY: Thanks, Stan, and hello to everyone back in the present. We've brought you here to 1803 to witness one of the true turning points in American history. As it happens, this one took place in Paris, France.

That's Monsieur Tallyrand, the French grand chamberlain, or treasurer. He's got a problem. The French are at war with England, and he has to find a way to pay for it.

(TALLYRAND'S SECRETARY brings a small table downstage and places it beside his boss. He unfolds a map and places it on the table. He continues to stand beside the table.)

SECRETARY: Monsieur Tallyrand, the American diplomat, James Monroe, is here to see you.

TALLYRAND: Thank you. Send him in.

(JAMES MONROE stands and comes downstage. He and TALLYRAND shake hands.)

MONROE: I'm honored to meet you, Mr. Foreign Minister. I bring compliments and greetings from President Jefferson. Sir, the president has authorized me to purchase the port of New Orleans from the French government for ten million dollars.

TALLYRAND: Yes, yes. I've given the matter careful consideration, and since our countries have always been friends and allies, I think we can come to an agreement. But perhaps we should think in larger terms.

MONROE: Sir?

TALLYRAND: How much would you give for the whole of Louisiana?

MONROE: (in surprise) The *whole* of Louisiana?

TALLYRAND: Here, sir— (He points to the map.) We are discussing that land stretching from the Mississippi River west to the Rocky Mountains, from the Gulf of Mexico to the Canadian border.

MONROE: Naturally, we're interested. However, I'll need time to discuss it with President Jefferson.

TALLYRAND: Yes, yes, of course. Take my offer to your president. But be quick about it, sir, before I decide to keep Louisiana.

(TALLYRAND and his SECRETARY exit. MONROE remains on stage poring over the map.)

HOLLY: Let's bring in our historical adviser, Dr. Osgood Conklin, and discuss this a little bit. Dr. Conklin, are you here?

(DR. CONKLIN enters from offstage.)

HOLLY: So you made it, Dr. Conklin.

CONKLIN: Good morning, Holly. Yes, it's very exciting for a historian to virtually go back in time.

HOLLY: What's your take on the Louisiana Purchase, Dr. Conklin? Did Americans get a good deal?

CONKLIN: Remember, when we say Louisiana we're not talking about the present-day state. We're talking about the whole middle part of the country. President Jefferson bought the Louisiana Territory for 15 million dollars, which comes to about four cents an acre.

HOLLY: So the United States doubled its land area in the stroke of a pen?

CONKLIN: Exactly. It was probably the greatest real estate deal in history. But you see, no one knew what was out there. The French, who owned it, didn't know, we didn't know. Only a few fur traders had ever set foot west of the Missouri River.

(MONROE exits with the map.)

HOLLY: Native Americans lived there. They certainly knew what was there.

CONKLIN: Yes, definitely, but there were many different tribes. This is a sad aspect of westward expansion. Remember, there had been many Indians east of the Mississippi River when the white colonists arrived. By about 1820, they had been largely displaced by whites. What's good for one group of people is often bad for another, and that was particularly true of whites and Indians.

HOLLY: We have Red Jacket, the eloquent Iroquois chief with us today. Let's hear what he had to say about the problem to President Washington in 1793.

(RED JACKET stands and steps downstage.)

RED JACKET: We first knew you as a feeble plant that wanted a little earth whereon to grow. We gave it to you, and afterward, when we could have trod you under our feet, we watered and protected you. Now you have grown into a mighty tree whose top reaches the clouds and whose branches overspread the whole land, whilst we, who were the tall pine of the forest, have become a feeble plant and need your protection.

(RED JACKET exits.)

CONKLIN: The mighty tree was growing even stronger. Native Americans west of the Mississippi River were about to experience firsthand what Red Jacket spoke of. Jefferson sent the Lewis and Clark expedition to explore not only the Louisiana Purchase but also the land west of Rockies, the Oregon Territory, and all the way to the Pacific Ocean.

Jefferson hoped they'd find a water route to the Pacific, thus linking both coasts, a northwest passage.

HOLLY: Did they find it?

CONKLIN: No, such a passage doesn't exist, but they got to the Pacific and back without losing a man. Even Lewis's Newfoundland dog made it back alive.

HOLLY: Let's listen to President Jefferson's instructions to Lewis and Clark in 1804.

(JEFFERSON stands and reads from his letter to the explorers.)

JEFFERSON: The object of your mission is to explore the Missouri River and communicate with the water of the Pacific Ocean. You will take observations of latitude and longitude at all remarkable points on the river. Copies of your observations and notes should be written on the paper of the birch tree as it is less liable to injury from the damp. Other objects worthy of notice will be: the soil and the face of the country, the animals, especially those not known in the U.S., the mineral production of every kind, the climate. You will establish friendly relations with the Indians who live there, and prepare the way for trade. You will determine, also, whether the land can accommodate a large population.

(JEFFERSON exits.)

HOLLY: So pioneering as we think of it began right there?

CONKLIN: Yes, but it took a while really to get started. Fur trappers followed Lewis and Clark into the Rocky Mountains, and many made fortunes. History is never black or white, positive or negative. The trappers wiped out entire animal populations, but as they did so, they explored the land, and they found routes that wagons could use. Jefferson thought the West was large enough to accommodate a thousand generations of settlers. He was wrong about that.

HOLLY: Was there one single reason why pioneers went west?

CONKLIN: There were several main reasons. Life was a lot harder in the nineteenth century. People didn't live very long. In one year alone, 1850, a cholera epidemic killed 30,000 people in the U.S. For a long time, more people died than were born, so some left to escape disease. And then there was the slavery problem.

HOLLY: How so?

CONKLIN: Many people thought slavery was immoral, and they wouldn't live near it. For others it was a matter of unfair competition. If we were neighbors, and you had twenty slaves on your farm, and I had none, you'd drive me out of business. I'd have to leave. Then, of course, in 1860 people went west to escape the Civil War. But that's getting ahead of ourselves, right?

HOLLY: That's right. We're visiting a pioneer family in Oregon in 1848.

CONKLIN: You're not going to tell them about the California gold strike in 1849, are you?

HOLLY: No, we're not allowed to divulge the future.

CONKLIN: Oh, good. But incidentally, in 1850, one year after the gold strike, 55,000 pioneers went west. That's more than during the entire 48 years since the Louisiana Purchase.

HOLLY: So the West grew crowded?

CONKLIN: Yes, and that's when trouble began between whites and Native Americans.

HOLLY: Let's go over to Stan to see how the trip west ended for one family.

(BLACKOUT. Sounds indicating time travel.)

(STAN enters.)

STAN: Thanks for that report, Holly, Dr. Conklin. He'll be joining us here in 1848. I hope. We lost him for a while last week in the Revolutionary War. This is the Foster family. They've kindly agreed to speak with us, to show us around the past.

(The FOSTERS stand as they're introduced, then join STAN downstage.)

This is Joseph Foster, his wife, Martha, their son, Owen, and their daughter, Emily. You folks have just arrived, I understand.

MARTHA: Yes, three weeks ago.

STAN: So here it is November tenth. When did you leave Missouri?

MARTHA: May the fourth.

STAN: Almost six months on the trail.

JOSEPH: We were lucky.

OWEN: We have a horse. He made it all the way.

STAN: Not many did, I hear.

MARTHA: Oxen are a lot heartier.

STAN: Where are you folks from?

MARTHA: Pennsylvania, then we moved to Kentucky, then Ohio.

STAN: You've moved a lot.

MARTHA: Joseph thinks the world's getting crowded if you can see your neighbor's chimney smoke.

OWEN: Me, too.

STAN: Where are your nearest neighbors now?

EMILY: We haven't seen anybody yet.

(DR. CONKLIN enters, looking around.)

STAN: Welcome, Doc. Meet the Fosters. Folks, this is Dr. Conklin. He's a historian.

EMILY: A what?

CONKLIN: A historian. That means I study the past.

STAN: This sure is a beautiful place you picked. How much land do you have?

JOSEPH: We get sixty acres for free from the government. But we don't own it outright until we've lived on it for six years.

CONKLIN: You know, the extraordinary thing about Oregon is that it's true wilderness, all 250,000 square miles of it. The Fosters are the first white people to see this place. Maybe the first people, period.

STAN: I notice you're plowing and planting before you've built a house.

JOSEPH: I guess you're not a farmer.

STAN: No, sir, I'm not.

OWEN: You got to get a crop of corn going before anything else.

JOSEPH: Son, these folks aren't from around here. They don't see things the same. Stan, we're used to living outdoors, but if we don't get in a crop we could starve next year. First things first.

MARTHA: We're pleased, though. Take a look at that soil under your feet.

CONKLIN: It just might be the most fertile soil on earth.

OWEN: Because of all the rain.

EMILY: I miss my friends.

STAN: From the wagon train?

EMILY: (nodding) They mostly went to Willamette Falls.

STAN: How far away is that?

EMILY: About a hundred miles.

MARTHA: We miss the society of people. Folks to chat with. Even Joseph misses company.

JOSEPH: They'll be coming—neighbors, even stores. People are pouring into Oregon country. You come back in five years, you won't recognize this place.

EMILY: We'll have a log cabin.

MARTHA: Maybe even a proper frame house with a floor.

JOSEPH: Right now all we can afford to think about is making it through the first winter.

STAN: What will you eat?

OWEN: We'll hunt. Next year I'll get my own gun, maybe.

JOSEPH: Yes, we've seen a fair quantity of game. And that stream's full of trout.

EMILY: I caught *three* fish yesterday.

MARTHA: Plus we bought some extra cornmeal and dried beef back at Fort Hall. It's clothes we're concerned about right now.

STAN: I thought you'd be wearing buckskins.

MARTHA: Well, we did, too.

JOSEPH: Martha made us buckskin pants and shirts back on the trail. But they didn't work so well in this climate.

CONKLIN: Too wet?

JOSEPH: They get pretty stiff after a couple of soakings.

OWEN: Stiff? I'll say. Like wearing stovepipes on your legs.

STAN: So what will you do?

MARTHA: I'll make overcoats out of the wagon cover. I also have two blankets I can cut up for cloth.

STAN: What about shoes?

Read-Aloud Plays: Pioneers Scholastic Professional Books

JOSEPH: I can make shoes. (The rest of the family rolls their eyes. JOSEPH grins.) Not great shoes, I admit. I haven't the skills to make right and left feet. Both shoes are the same. But they get wet a time or two, they begin to conform.

MARTHA: Would you gentlemen like to stay for dinner?

STAN: No, thank you. We'll have to be going.

JOSEPH: I guess we'd better get back to work, then.

STAN: Thank you for talking to us. We wish you good luck. You're very brave people.

JOSEPH: Brave? We're just doing what we must.

OWEN and EMILY: 'Bye. Come again.

(The FOSTERS take their seats upstage.)

STAN: How about that? They barely have enough for themselves, yet they invite us to dinner.

CONKLIN: A lot of good people went west, but there was something about pioneering that made people unusually helpful and generous.

STAN: Well, Doc, do you have anything to add before we head back?

CONKLIN: I'd like to pause briefly and look at this remarkable time and place we call nineteenth-century America. It was a period of dizzying change. In 1801, there were only 5,308,483 people in the U.S. One in five of those was enslaved. There were few good roads in the East, none in the West. Nothing—products, mail, people, nothing—moved faster than the speed of a horse. In the entire human history, nothing had ever moved faster. As we've seen, it took six months to get from Missouri to Oregon in 1850, but by 1880, most of the West had been settled by pioneers.

    If the Foster children live to be 40 years old, they will be able to cross the country by train in six days. Slavery will have been eradicated; so, unfortunately, will most of the Native Americans and the vast herds of animals Lewis and Clark had seen. If the Fosters live to be 60, they could own an automobile. And they could see airplanes fly.

STAN: Absolutely remarkable . . . such huge changes.

CONKLIN: Perhaps more changes than any other century in history.

STAN: Thank you, Doc. It's been a pleasure traveling with you. And now we'll head back to the present. I hope.

The Story Behind the Play

The United States was interested in acquiring the port of New Orleans because whoever possessed the city would also have the advantage in controlling the Mississippi River. Americans would then be able to ship their goods to markets. Why would France give up New Orleans? In the early 1800s, France and England were at war. France needed the money from the Louisiana Purchase to pay for the war. In addition, the English had defeated the French navy. It would be difficult and costly for the French to continue to hold New Orleans. On April 30, 1803, the United States gained 885,000 square miles of new territory with its purchase of Louisiana for $15 million.

In that same year, President Jefferson petitioned Congress for $2,500 to fund an overland expedition to explore the country west of the Mississippi River. Meriwether Lewis and William Clark were tapped to lead the expedition. Lewis and Clark crossed the Rockies and were within sight of the Pacific Ocean on November 7, 1805. The expedition "opened up" the West in many ways—there was interaction with Native American groups, the territory could be mapped reliably, new species of plants and animals were discovered, and Lewis and Clark's route became a trail for pioneers heading west.

BIBLIOGRAPHY

Bial, Raymond. *Frontier Home*. Boston: Houghton Mifflin, 1993.

Chu, Daniel, and Bill Shaw. *Going Home to Nicodemus: The Story of an African American Frontier Town and the Pioneers Who Settled It*. Morristown, NJ: Julian Messner, 1995.

Roop, Peter and Connie, eds. *Off the Map: The Journals of Lewis & Clark*. New York: Walker, 1993.

Activities

What Makes a Pioneer a Pioneer?

Pioneers create frontiers—places where civilization overtakes the wilderness. Voyagers such as Columbus may "discover" a place, expeditions such as those of Lewis and Clark may "explore" a place, but pioneers such as the Fosters in *Time Travel* move into the wilderness to live. They build houses and towns, and soon the frontier has disappeared. Begin a discussion by calling on students to define the words *pioneer* and *frontier*. As you read and perform the plays, ask students to reassess their definitions.

Real Estate for Sale

The French wanted to sell Louisiana in part because Napoleon was afraid that France would lose the territory to England. Share the following scenario with students: Suppose Tallyrand asked you to write a for-sale advertisement for Louisiana. He wants you to include facts such as the area of the purchase; the asking price; a description of the land, its inhabitants, and its climate; and a rough map.

Messages from the Past

Both Meriwether Lewis and William Clark kept detailed journals of their expedition. Urge students to do some time traveling and playwriting of their own and visit the expedition sometime between the years of 1804 and 1806. Many editions of the two explorers' journals are in print; instruct students to find passages that appeal to them. Then have them write and perform scenes for the play featuring Lewis, Clark, and/or any other members of their expedition, and Dr. Conklin, Stan, and Holly.

Express Mail

Until stagecoaches began carrying mail west in 1858, letters traveled from the East Coast to the West Coast by ship to Panama, overland across the isthmus, and by ship again to San Francisco. The Southern Overland Mail stagecoaches took 24 days to travel from St. Louis to San Francisco. The most famous Pony Express was established in 1860 but lasted only a little over a year (its owners lost more than $200,000). Riders traveled from St. Joseph, Missouri, to Sacramento, California, in 10 days. Encourage students to find out more about the people and names associated with the express, such as Stagecoach Mary Fields, Wells Fargo, John Butterfield, the "American Camel Express." You may also consider challenging them to plan and map sample express routes by sea and land from New York to San Francisco via Panama, by stagecoach from St. Louis to San Francisco in 24 days, or by horseback from St. Joseph to Sacramento in 10 days.

Letters Home

CAST

ANNIE, A girl traveling along the Oregon Trail

JOEY, Annie's older brother

10 WRITERS

MA, Annie and Joey's mother

DAD, Annie and Joey's father

WAGON MASTER

TOWNSPEOPLE Non-speaking roles

CAPTAIN, Leader of wagon train

MEMBERS OF WAGON TRAIN

WALTER JAMES, Fiddle player

INDIANS

TRAPPERS

MERCHANTS

Scene. 1850. Along the Oregon Trail. ANNIE and JOEY sit in chairs in the middle of the stage.

(The play is told in the form of letters written by ANNIE, JOEY, and other WRITERS. The WRITERS, with the rest of the non-speaking cast, will appear behind ANNIE and JOEY throughout the play and pantomime the action as the letters are read aloud. Read the play through several times and plan the action. The other WRITERS should step forward to stand beside ANNIE and JOEY when they speak.)

ANNIE: January 3, 1850

Dear Grandma,

Guess what, Grandma? We might be going to Oregon! Dad read a book about the West, and Ma says he's caught "Oregon fever." The book said Oregon was the Land of Milk and Honey, like that place in the Bible, I forget its name. Ma doesn't want to go. It takes months to get there, and she says what if her and Pa should die on the way, what would happen to us kids? Also, she doesn't want to give up our possessions that mean so much. You can't carry much in those wagons. You know that beautiful sideboard you gave us? Well, we couldn't take it. We couldn't even take our beds.

Dad says, look at it this way. Land is getting expensive here in Missouri. Joey will never be able to afford a farm of his own when he grows up. But in Oregon, the land is free. All you have to do is get there.

I don't know, but I think I agree with Ma. I don't want to go. Mainly because Ma says, if we went, we'd probably never see you again.

Love, Annie

JOEY: March 18, 1850

Dear Grandma,

It's decided, Grandma, we're going to Oregon! I think we're leaving in May. See, at that time the prairie grasses will have grown tall enough to feed the animals, and we'll get across the Rocky Mountains before winter. The Rocky Mountains—imagine that, Grandma. We're going to see Indians, too! We'll be crossing right over their land. Dad says they usually don't mind as long as you don't stop. He says they like to trade. Boy, would I like to have a pony.

Last week Dad and I went to buy a wagon. They call them "prairie schooners" because the white canvas tops look like sails on boats. We also bought eight oxen to pull it. I hoped we could get horses, but Dad says horses aren't strong enough to pull the wagon over the mountains.

Maybe you could come to Oregon with us.

Love, Joey

ANNIE: May 2, 1850

Dear Grandma,

You should have seen our send-off! The whole town of Springfield turned out to say good-bye. Stores closed and so did our school. Banners hung across the street. People made speeches. We're called emigrants. I looked it up. It means people who leave one country to go to another. That's us, all right. All our friends and classmates were crying and waving, and everyone wished us luck and gave us smoked hams and things. I cried, too. So did Ma. I looked back and waved until Springfield disappeared. I thought our wagon master (we call him the Captain) would make a speech, too. But he didn't, he just slapped the lead oxen on the rump and said "Git!"

So we've "git." We have been on the road for four days—no, five—and I guess I have to admit I'm excited. Not as excited as Joey and Dad, but more than Mom. Maybe Joey is right. Maybe this will be a great adventure. Miss you.

Love, Emigrant Annie

JOEY: May 10, 1850

Dear Grandma,

I'm sorry I didn't get to write sooner, but I've been learning to drive oxen. I'm a teamster. It's a lot of responsibility.

You should see us, Grandma. There are 90 wagons in our train. That's hundreds of people going west in our wagon train alone! A lot of wagons broke down during the first week, so we didn't get too far. Ours didn't break down. Now we're making about ten miles a day, the Captain says. I'll bet if you could see us from a bird's eye, we'd look like a great fleet of ships crossing the prairie. There are a lot of children Annie's age and some my age. We're both making new friends. This is the most fun I've ever had!

Love, Joey

ANNIE: May 16, 1850

Dear Grandma,

We're on the Great Plains now. There are no trees at all, nothing but grass as far as you can see. I don't like this place, Grandma. It's terribly hot, 100 degrees all day. We all suffer with it, but I think the animals suffer most of all. We're all exhausted, and we haven't even seen the mountains yet. How can we keep this up? Yet just when we think we can't, we see something beautiful. Like yesterday, we passed a giant field of purple wildflowers, it must have been five miles across. It was the most beautiful thing I've ever seen. I'll try to write more later, but my ink is drying up. I miss you.

Love, Annie

JOEY: May 24, 1850

Dear Grandma,

 It's hot! I was never so hot back home. Everything out here is bigger than anywhere I've ever been. The happy times are happier, and the miserable times are miserabler.

 This is how we spend every day on the plains. At 4 o'clock in the morning, the sentinels fire off their rifles, and everybody gets up and goes to work. Annie and Ma get a fire going, but there aren't any trees, so they got to use buffalo dung baked hard in the sun. Dad and I collect the animals, feed them, and hitch them up.

 We eat sowbelly and slamjacks for breakfast (that's bacon and pancakes) every day. Then we pack up and get ready to roll. At 7 o'clock, the Captain shouts, "Wagons, ho!" We got to be ready, because if you're late, you end up at the end of the wagon train, eating dust all day.

 Love, Joey

ANNIE: May 30, 1850

Dear Grandma,

 You wouldn't believe the noise we make as we get going each morning. Wagon wheels creak and screech, dogs bark, people shout at their animals, babies cry. Maybe you've heard us back in Missouri.

 Love, Annie

JOEY: June 6, 1850

Dear Grandma,

 Most people, except the real young and the real old, walk beside the wagons all day. Even people who have horses walk so as to save the animals for when we get to Oregon. Remember our ox, Spot? Well, he dropped dead yesterday. We all cried. We pulled out of line long enough to butcher him. He was a good ox, but he was tough, though.

 We stop for lunch at noon, but nobody unpacks the wagon to cook. We eat jerky standing up or sitting down in the shade of the wagons, if we can find any.

 Love, Joey

ANNIE: June 10, 1850

Dear Grandma,

 We've been traveling along the Platte River. The Platte must be the foulest tasting river in the West. Nobody can stand it, so we make it into coffee before we drink it. Even the animals drink coffee!

 The midday heat makes me stupid. We plod and creak along the ruts made by earlier wagon trains until about 7 o'clock. And then we circle the wagons, a great big circle about half the size of Independence, Missouri. We've gotten so good at it now that the last wagon perfectly completes the circle. We put the animals inside the circle so they don't wander off. People say it's also because of Indian attacks, but we haven't seen any Indians yet. Personally, I think the Indians have more sense than to live out here.

Love, Annie

JOEY: June 17, 1850

Dear Grandma,

Dad and I take care of the animals, while Ma and Annie cook dinner—Spot again tonight, but we're running out of Spot. The sunsets are beautiful, like the sun's saying, "Keep moving. It's even more beautiful out west."

Remember Walter James, who worked for the blacksmith? Turns out he plays the fiddle. It sure is sweet listening to his music before we go to bed. It doesn't matter that he can't play all the notes.

Love, Joey

ANNIE: June 20, 1850

Dear Grandma,

There's a lot of death out here. It's hard to get used to. Every day we pass graves and the skeletons of oxen, cows, and horses bleached white by the sun. I didn't know there would be so much death. Yesterday I saw a long braid of black woman's hair tangled in the grass. There was still a comb in it. There's no wood to make coffins, so people bury their dead as best they can. Wild animals dig up the bodies and eat them. I have nightmares about being pulled from my grave, but at least we've had only two deaths so far, and the Captain thought they would have died even if they'd stayed home.

Cholera, they say, is the worst. I hope we don't have any of that.

Love, Annie

WRITER 1: June 20, 1850: Today, 460 miles from where we started, we crossed the North Fork of the Platte River. It has a cantankerous reputation. Sometimes it's a half mile wide and six inches deep, but for us, it was deeper than a horse's head. We removed the wheels and made flat-bottom boats out of the wagons. Not good boats, but at least they floated. We were aided in this by the Captain, who showed us how to nail buffalo skins over the bottom of the wagon box to make it watertight. We lost not a single wagon. In fact, this crossing that we feared became a day of merriment and relief, which was a blessing, because everyone's getting tired.

WRITER 2: June 24, 1850: Today the Johansens' youngest daughter fell off their wagon, and the rear wheels ran over her legs. I saw it all, as our

wagon was next in line. The poor child gave out a hideous cry and then lay still. I averted my eyes, for I didn't want to see the terrible wounds, as I went to her. Her parents were screaming, their faces white as buffalo bones. We watched in wonder as the child stood up, brushed off her smock, and walked into her parents' arms. A miracle for which we can only thank God—and the spongy grasses on this side of the Platte. Had this happened on the other side, the Johansen girl would be nearing an agonizing death as I write this.

ANNIE: June 30, 1850

Dear Grandma,

The mountains, Grandma! We'll soon be off this terrible plain, not soon enough for me. I'm sure it'll be hard in the mountains, but at least there will be good water and cool days. And they say that the cholera can't live in the mountains. Maybe we'll get there without disease. The Captain says that'd make us an unusually lucky wagon train.

Love, Annie

WRITER 3: July 2, 1850: Since we crossed the Platte, the land has tilted against us. We climbed for three days steady to a crest beyond which the land dropped into a deep valley. The wonderful thing about this valley was that at its bottom there were trees! Shade. We haven't seen trees—or their shade—for almost two months. But first we had to get down the hill.

WRITER 4: July 6, 1850: We chained the wagon wheels so they couldn't turn, then with ropes we skidded the wagons down the hill. We lost five wagons when their ropes snapped. Their owners watched with unbelieving eyes as their homes tumbled end over end, disintegrating into splinters. The rest of us accommodated the homeless and their goods as best we could. They won't be left behind, anyway.

ANNIE: July 7, 1850

Dear Grandma,

It's called Ash Hollow, at the bottom of a scary hill, and it's the most beautiful place I've ever seen. But even if it isn't, it sure seems like it. I didn't know how much I loved trees until I was deprived of them. Sweet, cool streams run among the trees and wild roses. We swam in pools until we got too cold. Imagine that. Too *cold*. Why can't we make our new home right here?

Love, Annie

WRITER 5: July 10, 1850: We reached Fort Laramie two days ago, and I look forward to leaving. There are friendly Indians, wild fur trappers, and hostile merchants. One fellow, who wears a brace of pistols in his belt and a gold front tooth, makes his living by following the wagon trains up the steep trail to come. He collects the belongings emigrants discard to lighten their loads and brings them back to Fort Laramie to sell. If we have to abandon something, I'm going to bury it so this scoundrel can't profit from our loss.

JOEY: July 12, 1850
Dear Grandma,

Ma found a guidebook to the Oregon Trail. Here's what it said about Fort Laramie where we arrived yesterday: "You are now 640 miles from Independence, and it is discouraging to tell you that you have not yet traveled one third of the long road to Oregon." Ma fears more than one third of our endurance is spent, but I don't think so. We'll make it, I know we will.

Love, Joey

WRITER 6: July 19, 1850: Now we're climbing steadily, and the nights grow chilly. We're following the Sweetwater River up onto the spine of the Wind River Mountains. I don't know how the poor animals persevere.

ANNIE: July 23, 1850
Dear Grandma,

Everyone's animals are dying now with regularity. I feel sad for them. They came so far, tried so hard, but they didn't make it. I hope no one has reason to say the same about us.

Love, Annie

JOEY: July 25, 1850
Dear Grandma,

We crossed the Continental Divide today! Now all the rivers flow west. We'd heard so much about South Pass that I expected towering cliffs and deep gorges and things, but it turned out to be a gentle meadow. We crossed easily, and now we're at the eastern edge of the Oregon Territory.

You know what Dad said to me this morning? He said, "Son, you've grown up on this trip. It's time to stop to calling you Joey."

Love, Joseph

WRITER 6: August 3, 1850: We've reached Fort Bridger. We traded our poor worn-out oxen and some money for fresh oxen. That's how Jim Bridger makes money. He'll take our team, rest them up in good pasture, and then trade them to the next wagon train. They call these animals "recruited oxen." I wish I could recruit a new body for myself. Mine's about done in.

WRITER 7: August 19, 1850: The wagon train has split up now. About half the wagons headed for California, the rest of us on to Oregon. We had a big party the night before we split. We have much to celebrate, mostly that the cholera spared us, but it's also sad.

WRITER 8: September 1, 1850: We've made friends we'll never forget, but now they're gone. We almost changed our minds and went to California with the others after hearing how the men at Fort Hall raved about California as the Promised Land. And they told us how dreadful the trail to Oregon would get. Then the Captain explained that those men work for the Hudson's Bay Company, and their furs come from Oregon, so of course they don't want it settled by farmers like us. Live and learn.

ANNIE: September 7, 1850

Dear Grandma,

    We've been talking so much about crossing the Continental Divide that I began to think of that as the end, but we still have 600 miles to go. They will sorely test us all. Nobody says it out loud, at least not the grown-ups, but everybody's frightened of what lies ahead.

    Love, Annie

WRITER 9: September 21, 1850: We've traveled 200 miles along the Snake River. No one has died along this stretch. The Captain says that makes us about the luckiest wagon train in history. Beyond the Snake River lie the Blue Mountains, then the Cascades, then the Columbia River. Will our luck hold all that way?

JOEY: October 2, 1850

Dear Grandma,

    No sooner, it seems, do we cross one range than another rears up before us. We have to stop to push great boulders aside or chop through brush and trees. Sometimes we have to unload all the wagons, and us men pull them up the trail by ropes. We load them up again, go a half mile, and do it all over. As a result, we cover no more than three miles a day. Everyone pitches in to help, though, and we feel good about that.

    Love, Joseph

WRITER 9: October 5, 1850: We must make a decision now. How to get across the Cascade Mountains? We hear about a new wagon route—

WRITER 10: But it is said to be steep and broken. The alternative is by water. We'd abandon our wagons and build rafts or boats and float right down the Columbia River—

Read-Aloud Plays: Pioneers Scholastic Professional Books

WRITER 9: That would certainly be a change, but it's 230 miles. I've never been much of a sailor, and I hear there are rapids.

JOEY: October 19, 1850

Dear Grandma,

   We've been riding the Columbia River for two weeks now. It's beautiful but dangerous. That's true of a lot of places out west. Our provisions are about gone. We're hungry all the time. They say that if one of us emigrants isn't hungry, then he's sick. I added it up today— we've been on the trail for four days short of six months.

   Love, Joseph

WRITER 2: October 23, 1850: Tragedy befell us today. Remember the Johansen girl who was run over by her wagon? Her parents were drowned when their raft overturned in rapids. Their young daughter, who was on another raft, survived. Since the wife and I have no children, we offered to take her on to Oregon. Her name is Ilsa. If she wants to stay on with us, well, that would be fine, poor child.

ANNIE: November 9, 1850

Dear Grandma,

   We're here! We made it! We picked a beautiful place near a fine stream. It's all forest now, of course, but soon it will be our new home. Want to hear something funny? In order to have shelter while we get a crop planted, we bought a wagon from a family who took the overland route. It feels pretty familiar. We're not emigrants anymore!

   Love, Annie

The Story Behind the Play

Along with the Santa Fe Trail to New Mexico, the Oregon Trail was a major route to the west. Both trails also branched off to California. The advantages of the Oregon Trail included water in the form of the Missouri, Blue, Platte, Sweetwater, Bear, Boise, and Snake rivers, and easy fording across them; the grass of the Great Plains for livestock; and low passes through the mountains. On average, the 2,000-mile trek along the Oregon Trail took from four to six months to complete. In places, its path stretched to a width of 20 miles.

In the spring of 1842, the first wagon train left Independence, Missouri, and made its way along the Oregon Trail. About 1,000 people made the journey that year. Almost that many, 875, headed west on the trail in the following year. The numbers increased to about 1,400 in 1844 and 3,000 in 1845. With the opening of the transcontinental railroad in 1869, traffic along the Oregon Trail decreased, but it was still in use as late as the 1880s.

BIBLIOGRAPHY

Conrad, Pam. *Prairie Songs*. New York: Harper, 1985.

Fisher, Leonard. *The Oregon Trail*. New York: Holiday, 1990.

Freedman, Russell. *Children of the Wild West*. New York: Clarion Books, 1983.

Rounds, Glen. *The Prairie Schooners*. New York: Holiday House, 1994.

Sigerman, Harriet. *Land of Many Hands: Women in the American West*. New York: Oxford University Press, 1997.

Activities

On the Oregon Trail

Wagon trains could travel about 10 miles a day. At that rate of speed, about how long would a trip along the Oregon Trail take? How long would the same trip take with today's speed limits? Guide students in finding maps of the Oregon Trail. Then have them determine its length and compare the amount of time a trip in 1850 would take with a trip in 1999.

Voices from the West

Many pioneers kept diaries and journals as they traveled west along the Oregon Trail. Ask students to find one or two diary entries that they especially like and then hold a "Westward Ho!" reading. Your class may want to invite other classes and family and friends to the reading.

Just Fiddlin' Around

Walter James and his fiddle entertained Annie and Joey and the other members of the wagon train. What songs were popular in the mid-1800s as pioneers traveled along the trails? What songs were influenced by the pioneer movement? After students research the songs of the time, suggest that they form one or more wagon train bands. Set aside time for the bands to perform their favorite songs.

Sailing Across the Plains

Prairie schooners measured 4 feet by 10 feet. When loaded, the wagons could weigh from 3,000 to 7,000 pounds. Pioneers had to pack all the necessities of home, including the following recommended food supplies per person: 200 lb flour, 75 lb bacon, 30 lb pilot bread, 5 lb coffee, 2 lb tea, 25 lb sugar, ½ bushel dried beans, 1 bushel dried fruit, 2 lb saleratus (baking soda), 10 lb salt, ½ bushel cornmeal, ¼ bushel parched or ground corn, and 1 keg vinegar. Divide the class into groups of four or five students and challenge them to pack for a six- to seven-month-long journey along the Oregon Trail. They should begin by making a list of what they would carry. Let them mark off a wagon's dimensions on the classroom floor with masking tape or make a scale model on graph paper.

Every Landmark Tells a Story

Council Bluffs, Chimney Rock, Independence Rock, South Pass, Fort Laramie, Soda Springs, and the Snake River are just a few of the landmarks along the Oregon Trail. Direct students to draw story maps based on the play. The maps should show the route of the Oregon Trail; the landmarks mentioned by Annie, Joey, and the other writers; and the significance of the landmark to the characters in the play. Students may also locate and label other landmarks and write brief letters about the places to include in the play.

The Shortcut

CAST

Members of a wagon train traveling along the Oregon Trail

MR. CONNOR
MRS. CONNOR
LIZZY CONNOR, age 13

MR. PRESTWICK
MRS. PRESTWICK
JACOB PRESTWICK, age 12

MR. LARSEN
MRS. LARSEN
ERIC LARSEN, age 15

MR. HELMSETTER
MRS. HELMSETTER
SOPHIE HELMSETTER, age 12

CAPTAIN, Leader of the wagon train

Another pioneer family
MR. OSWALD
MRS. OSWALD
MARY OSWALD, age 14

JIM BRIDGER, A mountain man

PIONEERS

TRADERS at Fort Laramie

NATIVE AMERICANS

Act 1

SCENE 1. Late spring, 1853. A wagon train on the western edge of the Great Plains. It is evening. The snow-capped Rocky Mountains are in sight, stage right. The CONNOR, PRESTWICK, LARSEN, and HELMSETTER families are on stage. They are having a meeting.

MR. CONNOR: I've been doing some figuring. At this rate, we won't make Oregon before the middle of October. How many wagon trains do you reckon have come before us?

MR. PRESTWICK: (shrugs) Don't know . . . maybe ten years' worth.

MR. CONNOR: That's my point. All those folks have picked the best land in Oregon. What will be left for us if we don't get there till autumn?

MRS. LARSEN: Just what are you proposing, Mr. Connor?

MR. CONNOR: This right here. (He takes a folded, dog-eared paper from his pocket and passes it around.)

MR. HELMSETTER: (turning the paper this way and that) What is this?

MR. CONNOR: Why, it's a map. A map of a shortcut.

MRS. LARSEN: A shortcut? You know how the Captain feels about shortcuts.

MR. CONNOR: Well, maybe the Captain doesn't even know about this shortcut. It says right there that the shortcut chops 150 miles off the route.

MR. LARSEN: (studying the map) Bridger's Pass . . .

MR. CONNOR: (impatiently taking the map) Look, here's South Pass, the one we're aiming for. And here's Bridger's Pass. You can see that Bridger's Pass takes a more direct route over the mountains.

LIZZY CONNOR: You mean we'd leave the wagon train, Pa?

MR. CONNOR: Lizzy, what I'm saying is we *all* ought to take this shortcut.

LIZZY: But, Pa, we can't—

MR. HELMSETTER: (shaking his head) The Captain will never agree.

MR. CONNOR: Aren't we free men? Isn't it our right to take whatever route suits us? We're not in the army.

MRS. LARSEN: I guess we got a right—as far as that goes.

MR. CONNOR: One hundred and fifty miles. Just think, we make about ten or twelve miles a day. That's almost two weeks we'd save!

(Silence. Everyone wants to travel faster, but they are full of misgivings.)

MR. CONNOR: The Prestwicks are all for it, aren't you?

MR. PRESTWICK: I just don't know—

MR. CONNOR: What? You were all for it yesterday.

MR. PRESTWICK: Yesterday we were just talking. That's different from actually doing it.

MR. HELMSETTER: I'd better go and get the Captain.

(MR. HELMSETTER exits stage left.)

LIZZY: Pa, I don't want to leave our friends.

MR. CONNOR: Don't worry, Lizzy. When we get to Fort Laramie, we'll meet other families who'll want to take the Bridger's Pass shortcut. You'll meet new friends.

LIZZY: But, Pa, I don't want—

(MR. HELMSETTER enters stage left with the CAPTAIN.)

CAPTAIN: Evening, folks. What's up?

MR. HELMSETTER: Mr. Connor wants to take a shortcut.

CAPTAIN: A *what*?

MR. CONNOR: That's right, Captain. Look at this map. Show him the map.

(Whoever has the map now passes it to the CAPTAIN. He studies it.)

CAPTAIN: Where'd you get this?

MR. CONNOR: From a man in Independence, Missouri. He said the man who gave it to him got it from Jim Bridger himself.

CAPTAIN: Kids, what are the first two rules of wagon training? Sophie?

SOPHIE: Keep moving—

ERIC: And don't take no shortcuts.

CAPTAIN: That's right. Now, folks, look at those mountains. They aren't like any mountains back east. They're tough in *fine* weather. In the winter, eighteen feet of snow falls up there, fifty degrees below zero is common, and the wind'll cut you like a sword. You know what'd happen if you took a bad trail and got stuck up there for the winter?

JACOB: What, Captain?

CAPTAIN: Why, son, your body'd have a race with itself.

JACOB: A race?

CAPTAIN: Yep, a race. Between starvin' to death and freezin' to death. Now let's not have any more talk about shortcuts.

(BLACKOUT)

SCENE 2. The same evening after dinner. LIZZY CONNOR, ERIC LARSEN, and SOPHIE HELMSETTER are on stage by themselves, staring at the mountains.

LIZZY: Look how the moon shines on the snow. (shivering) It looks like bones. My father means to take that shortcut despite what the Captain said.

SOPHIE: Grown-ups can be so stubborn.

ERIC: Maybe it's a good shortcut.

LIZZY: I have a bad feeling about it.

ERIC: The Captain was telling me about that Jim Bridger. He's a mountain man. Did you know that the Captain used to be a mountain man? They explored the Rockies together, the first white men who ever saw the "wondrous sights." That's what the Captain called them— wondrous. I hope it's not too late for me to be a mountain man.

SOPHIE: The mountains will still be there after we're long gone.

LIZZY: Maybe when you're a mountain man, Eric, you'll find our bones under fifteen feet of snow on the shortcut.

SOPHIE: Oh Lizzy, don't say things like that even as a joke.

LIZZY: Who's joking?

(JACOB PRESTWICK enters.)

JACOB: (to LIZZY) Your father has about convinced my father to take that shortcut. I wish your father would just shut up.

Read-Aloud Plays: Pioneers Scholastic Professional Books

LIZZY: I wish he would, too.

JACOB: (gloomily) Want some licorice?

SOPHIE: Licorice? You have licorice?

JACOB: Shhh! Not so loud. I've been hoarding it.

(He passes it around.)

JACOB: It's pretty much melted.

LIZZY: It's wondrous.

JACOB: I wonder which would win.

ERIC: What?

JACOB: Freezin' or starvin'.

ERIC: Oh. Freezing.

(The CAPTAIN enters.)

CAPTAIN: Evening, kids. What's up?

ERIC: We're watching the mountains.

CAPTAIN: Yep, for mountains, they don't come any better than that.

LIZZY: Captain, Jacob and I don't want to take any shortcuts. We're scared.

CAPTAIN: Now don't you worry about that.

LIZZY: Don't worry? Why not?

CAPTAIN: We'll be in Fort Laramie day after tomorrow. Don't you worry, Lizzy.

LIZZY: You don't know my father—

CAPTAIN: That wouldn't be licorice, would it?

JACOB: Oh. Yes. Have some.

CAPTAIN: (winking) I sure do like licorice.

(The kids stare at the CAPTAIN, trying to figure out what he's got up his sleeve.)

Act 2

SCENE. A few days later in Fort Laramie. This is the last bit of civilization the pioneers will see before they set out over the Rockies, which will be the hardest and most dangerous part of the entire trip. The PRESTWICKS, LARSENS, and HELMSETTERS are on stage. They are talking quietly about their plans. The kids are walking around the fort. LIZZY CONNOR is with them, but her parents are offstage. Pioneers, traders, and Native Americans are upstage, buying and selling and trading.

LIZZY: Civilization feels funny after being on the trail for so long.

SOPHIE: I know. Don't buildings seem like strange things?

ERIC: Did you see all those mountain men? They must be having some kind of get-together.

(They come upon MARY OSWALD, who is strolling by herself.)

LIZZY: Hey.

MARY: Hey, yourself.

LIZZY: I'm Lizzy. This is Eric, Jacob, and Sophie.

(They say hello and shake hands.)

LIZZY: Are you joining our wagon train?

MARY: I guess not. My pa wants to take this shortcut—

LIZZY: He *does*?

MARY: He let our wagon train leave without us a week ago. We're leaving tomorrow.

(MR. CONNOR enters leading MARY's parents, MR. and MRS. OSWALD.)

MR. CONNOR: Folks, could I have your attention?

(The CAPTAIN and JIM BRIDGER enter from the other side of the stage, but they hang back as the others gather around MR. CONNOR.)

ERIC: (nudging JACOB) Look at that guy with the Captain. There's a mountain man if I ever saw one—

MR. CONNOR: This is Mr. and Mrs. Oswald.

MRS. OSWALD: And that's our daughter, Mary.

Read-Aloud Plays: Pioneers Scholastic Professional Books

MR. CONNOR: Mr. Oswald and I got to talking, and it turns out he has the same map of Bridger's Pass shortcut as me.

MR. OSWALD: Yes sir, that's right. My old friend got this map from Jim Bridger himself. Bridger told him it was a foolproof shortcut, easier than South Pass itself. *And* it's 200 miles shorter.

BRIDGER: (stepping into the semicircle) Excuse me, Mr. Oswald, but I couldn't help overhearing. You say Jim Bridger himself—the toughest, smartest, fastest, straight-shootin'est, slap-dab greatest all-around mountain man in the entire world gave your friend that map?

MR. OSWALD: Yes sir, I—

BRIDGER: And you say this fellow Bridger told your friend he ought to take this shortcut?

MR. OSWALD: Yes sir, he did. And who might you be, sir?

BRIDGER: Who *might* I be? I'd *be* Jim Bridger himself.

MR. CONNOR: Jim—?

ERIC: Wow! Really!

BRIDGER: May I have a squint at that map?

(MR. CONNOR hands the map to BRIDGER.)

BRIDGER: Yep, that's my map, all right. Yep. Been up there twice. Since I was the first, I named it after myself.

MR. OSWALD: Would you lead us over Bridger's Pass? We can pay.

BRIDGER: Nope.

MR. CONNOR: No? Just like that? Why not?

BRIDGER: You all can take Bridger's Pass by yourselves. All's you have to do is follow my map. That is, if you mean to kill your families and commit suicide yourselves.

MR. CONNOR: What do you mean?

BRIDGER: I *mean* it ain't no proper trail at all. Nothin' but a narrow path wide enough for a man on horseback, with a thousand-foot drop on either side. *I* almost died up there one winter. You folks in wagons will get stuck, and you'll start to starve—if the cold don't kill you first. So there's your choice. You can stay with my friend the Captain and get to Oregon in due time, or you can take Bridger's Pass and not get there at all. (He turns to walk away.)

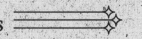

MR. CONNOR: Mr. Bridger!

BRIDGER: Yes, sir?

MR. CONNOR: I—I want to thank you. I'm glad you happened to be here.

BRIDGER: You can thank the Captain for that. He rode ahead to ask me to wait.

MR. CONNOR: Captain, I apologize. You're the leader, and you won't hear nothing more from me.

CAPTAIN: Apology accepted, Mr. Connor.

BRIDGER: (turning to ERIC) Son.

ERIC: Who me? Yes, sir?

BRIDGER: What's the first two rules of wagon training?

ERIC: Keep moving—

THE OTHER KIDS: (in unison) AND DON'T TAKE ANY SHORTCUTS!

The Story Behind the Play

Jim Bridger was born in Virginia in 1804, the same year that Lewis and Clark started on their expedition to the West. Orphaned at the age of 13, Bridger was apprenticed to a blacksmith for several years until he answered a newspaper advertisement for "enterprising young men" to hunt and trap on the Missouri River. He is credited with being the first white man to reach the Great Salt Lake in 1824.

Although Bridger's Pass in this play is fictional, the Donner Party has gone down in history for taking a real shortcut called the "Hastings Shortcut," with tragic results. They were stranded at the Truckee Pass in the Sierra Nevadas by winter blizzards. Of the 87 people in the party, 47 survived. Donner's daughter Virginia later wrote this piece of advice on pioneering to an eastern cousin, "Never take no cut offs and hurry along as fast as you can."

Built originally by the American Fur Company in 1834, Fort Laramie was eventually purchased by the army. Trappers sold or traded their furs for the necessities of wilderness life such as flour, dried meats, gunpowder, and ammunition. Pioneers bound for Oregon stopped to rest, refill their depleted larders, and refit their wagons. Indians also come to trade. As a result of this traffic, the fort resembled a miniature town, with a general store, blacksmiths, livery stables, and so on.

BIBLIOGRAPHY

Calvert, Patricia. *Great Lives: The American Frontier*. New York: Atheneum, 1997.

Erickson, Paul. *Daily Life in a Covered Wagon*. Washington, DC: Preservation Press, 1994.

Levine, Ellen. . . . *If You Traveled West in a Covered Wagon*. New York: Scholastic, 1992.

Steedman, Scott. *A Frontier Fort on the Oregon Trail*. New York: Peter Bedrick Books, 1993.

Activities

Saving Steps

General Grenville M. Dodge said this about Jim Bridger: "He could make a map of any country he had ever traveled over, mark out its stream, mountains and obstacles correctly." Challenge students' mapmaking skills by asking them to draw maps of the school, neighborhood, or town and then figure out a shortcut between two locations. If it's feasible, have them try their shortcuts to determine how much time and distance the new routes really save.

Lizzy's Letter

As it turned out, Lizzy Connor's misgivings about the shortcut were well-founded. Ask students what arguments Lizzy could have made to convince her father not to take the shortcut. They may present their arguments in the form of letters or speeches. You may also want to have some students take on the role of Mr. Connor and have them respond to Lizzy's arguments.

Truth or Tall Tale?

Some of the real adventures of pioneers seem almost too fantastic to be true. Legends have also grown up around mountain men such as Mike Fink, who was a trapper with Jim Bridger. Guide students in compiling a list of characters in American tall tales—Paul Bunyan, Mike Fink, Pecos Bill, and so on. Encourage them to play detectives and discover the "truth" behind the tales. Good resources are *Cut from the Same Cloth* by Robert San Souci and *Who'd Believe John Colter?* by Mary Blount Christian.

Meet the Mountain Men (and Women)

Jim Bridger, Jim Beckwourth, Manuel Lisa, and Jedediah Smith have gone down in history as mountain men. Women such as Isabella Bird are known for their adventures in the West as well. Discuss and list the characteristics students think a mountain man or woman would possess. Then have them do research on these western adventurers.

The Cake Wreck

CAST

NARRATOR, She is MARY PIERCE as an older woman looking back on her pioneer experiences

CORDELIA PIERCE, Mary's mother

SIDNEY PIERCE, Mary's father

MARY PIERCE, The NARRATOR as a 10-year-old girl

MATTY PIERCE, Mary's older brother

UNCLE FRANK, The Pierces' neighbor; Aunt Sarah's husband

AUNT SARAH, the Pierces' neighbor; Uncle Frank's wife

TED TIGER, Seminole and neighbor

LITTLE TED, Ted's son, about Matty's age

Act 1

SCENE. Southeast Florida in 1878, near present-day Palm Beach. The PIERCES' one-room house. It is built of lumber they have found on the nearby beach. The roof is made of thatch from a local plant called palmetto. The furniture is homemade. There is a fireplace also used as a cooking stove. The NARRATOR is seated in a chair at stage right.

NARRATOR: Everything's different now, of course. Why, we have paved roads and passenger trains that actually stop. There's a real town. It's no great shakes by most standards, but we have stores where you can buy most anything a person might need, there's schools for kids of all ages, and even a library. And right now they're building another hotel. That'll make two hotels. Imagine that—tourists in Palm Beach, Florida, enough for *two* hotels.

Old people are always saying to young people, "Why, when I was your age, so on and so forth." I don't want to be another of those, but, golly, everything was *so* different back then that you might be interested in hearing about it—about how we lived.

(A family of four appears on stage—CORDELIA and SIDNEY PIERCE and their two children, MATTY and his sister, the young MARY.)

NARRATOR: My family—the Pierces—were just the third family to settle on the beach.

(MATTY puts something slimy and crawly down MARY's back. She squeals and takes a swing at him.)

NARRATOR: He was always doing that kind of thing to me. Everyone thinks of pioneers as being the people who went west in covered wagons. We were pioneers no less than them. When we came to south Florida in 1875, this piece of beach between West Palm Beach and Fort Lauderdale was the most remote place on the whole East Coast.

UNCLE FRANK: (from offstage) Wreck on the beach! Wreck on the beach!

NARRATOR: I should tell you something about this wreck business because it will seem unusual to modern-day folks. The thing that made this part of Florida so remote was the fact that there were no harbors. Just a beach, a hundred miles of unbroken beach. Things wash up on a beach like that. Thousands of different things. There were no stores back then; you couldn't buy what you needed. Without beachcombing, we wouldn't have made it down here. Sometimes things would just wash up, you'd never know from where. Rarely did we ever see an actual shipwreck, but this time we did.

UNCLE FRANK: (from offstage) Wreck on the beach!

NARRATOR: There's just one more thing I want to tell you. There's a law of the sea called "salvage." The law says anything you find from a wreck is yours to keep. Too, if we didn't take the things the sea cast up, the sea would just take them back.

(The PIERCES all move at once, pulling on their jackets and hats. SIDNEY opens the door for UNCLE FRANK.)

UNCLE FRANK: Evening, evening one and all. Well, she's come ashore. She's breaking up right now.

CORDELIA: Did the crew get off safely?

UNCLE FRANK: That other steamship took everybody off this morning, and then it left. I guess they couldn't repair her in this wind, so they left her at anchor. They must have known it wouldn't hold.

SIDNEY: Probably didn't have any other choice.

UNCLE FRANK: Trouble is, the sky's looking distinctly unfriendly. At least the wind keeps the mosquitoes down. They were getting awful bad. I just hope it's not a hurricane.

CORDELIA: Do you think it might be?

UNCLE FRANK: Here we are in late August. The time's surely right.

SIDNEY: Then we better hurry.

CORDELIA: Maybe we ought to wait.

NARRATOR: None of us had ever seen a hurricane then. We'd heard a lot about them, but hearing isn't the same as seeing.

SIDNEY: There's no telling where things'll be after the storm. That linen you wanted, Cordy, it could be under six feet of sand. And I bet that poor ship was just full of linen. Not to mention muslin—

MARY: And felt—

SIDNEY: Oh, lots of felt.

CORDELIA: All right, all right. There are things we need, that's for sure. But at the first sign of weather, we drop everything and head back here. Agreed?

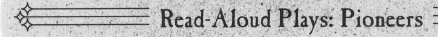

UNCLE FRANK: Here comes Ted Tiger. Let's hear what he has to say.

(TED TIGER and his son LITTLE TED enter. Everyone greets them.)

NARRATOR: A community of Seminole Indians lived out west of us on the other side of Lake Worth. One thing most people don't know about Seminole is they weren't from Florida any more than we were. They came from North Carolina after a war between Indians, so they were pioneers just like us, except they came a hundred years earlier. We all got along well. My mother taught Ted Tiger and Little Ted to read English.

(The actors freeze to indicate that a flashback is taking place. TED TIGER, LITTLE TED, and CORDELIA step downstage.)

TED: Mrs. Pierce, last night I saw the future in a dream. It said, "Ted Tiger, many white people will come before ten seasons pass. You'd better know how to read their writing." If you teach me and Little Ted to read your language, I'll bring you six buckskins and a canoe.

CORDELIA: It would be my pleasure. But we have only two books.

NARRATOR: And, boy, did they learn fast, because the future was coming fast.

(TED TIGER, LITTLE TED, and CORDELIA join the others.)

TED: We're returning your book—

SIDNEY: How many times have you read that book?

(TED and his son confer.)

LITTLE TED: Nine times.

MATTY: You can always borrow the other one.

SIDNEY: Maybe there's a beach full of books.

CORDELIA: Ted, is a hurricane coming?

TED: Yes, I think so. It should hit when the sun is higher.

SIDNEY: We'd better get moving, then.

(The kids agree enthusiastically and start offstage.)

CORDELIA: Wait! We all stay together. Understood?

(They agree, nodding their heads—anything to get going.)

MATTY: Hey, Teddy, wait up!

(Everyone hurries offstage to the wreck.)

NARRATOR: (shaking her head and sighing) We didn't know. We just didn't know.

(BLACKOUT)

Act 2

SCENE. Later that day, in the PIERCES' home. It is empty. We hear the sound of wind, not strong wind, not yet, but audible. The actors could experiment with ways to imitate the changing sound of wind as its speed increases. **A theatrical hint:** The sound effects should *imitate* the wind, not necessarily *duplicate* it. We hear noises offstage—thunks and such—the sound of heavy things being moved.

(CORDELIA, SIDNEY, and MARY enter carrying goods from the wreck. Among other things, CORDELIA has found a crate of cloth with which to make clothes, and she is delighted. MARY has found a doll dressed in the clothes of the day, some wooden toys, and anything else the students think of.)

NARRATOR: It's hard for people today to imagine how important those bits of civilization were to us then. It's hard even for me to remember, now that I can go to a store and buy things. I take them for granted, sometimes.

SIDNEY: Lumber! I found lumber!

CORDELIA: Isn't it wonderful!

SIDNEY: I can put a proper roof on this place, instead of palmetto thatch.

CORDELIA: Imagine—a roof that doesn't leak! I've forgotten what a dry house is like.

(UNCLE FRANK enters with crates.)

UNCLE FRANK: Look! Look at this! Butter. Sugar. Flour. Coffee. Crates and crates of it!

NARRATOR: That came to be known as the Cake Wreck, because it gave us the ingredients to make cakes. That was the only time in my whole childhood that we had more than we needed. We kept everything fresh by burying it.

(The wind increases.)

UNCLE FRANK: (looking worried) I'd better be getting back to my place. It's comin' on to blow.

CORDELIA: Wait a minute! Where's Matty?

SIDNEY: Wasn't he with you?

CORDELIA: I thought he was with you—

MARY: He wasn't with me.

CORDELIA: No! Oh, no!

(CORDELIA, SIDNEY, and UNCLE FRANK rush offstage, calling for MATTY. MARY is alone onstage as the wind builds. She's growing more and more frightened. Suddenly she rushes offstage to join them.)

NARRATOR: The sky turned a terrible shade of green, then it went black as night, like nature took it in her head to destroy every living thing in the world.

(BLACKOUT)

(The wind howls. It is at its peak now. After a few moments, the lights come back on. CORDELIA, SIDNEY, and MARY return—without MATTY. MARY is trying not to cry.)

SIDNEY: It's all my fault. You said we should wait. It's all my fault.

CORDELIA: We got so excited about those *things* that we lost sight of each other.

SIDNEY: We got greedy.

CORDELIA: He'll be all right. He *has* to be all right.

SIDNEY: Sure, Matty's a smart boy. Maybe he's with one of the other families or with Ted Tiger's people.

CORDELIA: Sure. What do the Seminole do in hurricanes? They live in those open huts, those chickees. They've been through this kind of storm before. They made it.

SIDNEY: We'll be lucky if this place holds up—

UNCLE FRANK: (offstage, shouting) Pierces! Pierces! Help!

(SIDNEY opens the door; the wind sound suddenly increases. UNCLE FRANK and AUNT SARAH enter huddled under whatever clothes they could tie around themselves. SIDNEY fights to close the door after them, and the sound diminishes.)

SARAH: It's gone! Our home is completely gone!

UNCLE FRANK: We were lucky to get out alive—

SARAH: The wind blew so hard the rain couldn't run down the wall. It just stuck there to the outside!

UNCLE FRANK: Yeah, until the wall came down!

SARAH: (looking around) Where's your boy? Where's Matty?

(Everyone is silent for a moment.)

SARAH: Don't tell me—

CORDELIA: Oh, Sarah, he's out there somewhere.

SIDNEY: We got separated on the beach.

NARRATOR: We all huddled in the corner and waited, hoping that Matty was safe and that the house wouldn't blow down. There was nothing else we could do.

(BLACKOUT)

Act 3

SCENE. A few hours later inside the PIERCES' home.

CORDELIA: Is it passing? Listen—

SIDNEY: Yes! Yes, the wind's down.

SARAH: Thanks be for that.

CORDELIA: It's passing—the rain has stopped.

(They all stand and go to the door to look out.)

NARRATOR: I'd never seen anything like that destruction. The jungle was stripped bare of leaves. The ocean was in our front yard.

(They close the door. SIDNEY puts a consoling arm around CORDELIA, who's trying to be strong.)

SIDNEY: We can go out soon. We'll find him. I promise we'll find him.

CORDELIA: I wish I never seen these, these—*goods*!

SIDNEY: Me, too.

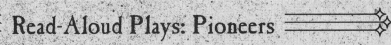

(There are noises outside. Everyone runs to open the door. MATTY enters, followed by LITTLE TED.)

MATTY: You're all safe! I was afraid the house would blow away!

SIDNEY: *You* were afraid? (starting to laugh in relief) How about that? He was afraid for *us*!

MATTY: You know what we did? Little Ted pulled his dugout up on the shore and turned it upside down. We climbed under it, and the wind didn't even get to us. We were hiding under there, and the wind was blowing so loud you couldn't hear yourself think, and then Little Ted shouted, "Well, at least there's no mosquitoes."

(Everyone laughs, and Little Ted looks embarrassed but pleased.)

CORDELIA: Little Ted, I'd like to give you a gift for saving my boy. (She picks up the other book and hands it to LITTLE TED.) It's a little wet, but I'd like you to have this for your own.

NARRATOR: The next day after we'd cleaned up some of the mess, we made cakes. How we enjoyed that little luxury. Ted and his family, too. They'd never had cake before. As years passed and new families came down, we'd tell them about the wreck and the wind. Uncle Frank would always tell it the same way. He'd say, "It blew a crooked road straight and scattered the days of the week so bad that Sunday didn't come around until Tuesday morning." (nodding to herself) And that's exactly what it felt like, too.

(BLACKOUT)

The Story Behind the Play

In the early 1700s, English settlers began moving into Muskogee territory in what is now Georgia and Alabama. Because the Muskogee lived along creeks and river, the English called them Creeks. Many Muskogee moved into present-day Florida, which was then controlled by Spain. This group became known as Seminoles. In the early 1800s, American settlers again began encroaching upon Seminole territory. Conflicts between the Americans and the Seminole led to the First Seminole War. By the close of the war, Spain had sold Florida to the United States. The Seminole had been forced south, but their new lands were protected by a treaty with the American government. The treaty didn't deter settlement, and conflicts continued to arise.

In 1828 President Andrew Jackson signed the Indian Removal Act with the aim of removing all the Native Americans in the Southeast to new lands in the West. Under the leadership of Osceola, some Seminole refused to leave Florida. The Second Seminole War began. This war, which never officially ended, resulted in great losses to both sides. Thousands of Seminole were sent to Oklahoma. However, a few hundred moved deeper into the Everglades and settled there. Florida was admitted into the United States in 1845 as a slave-holding state, seceded from the Union in 1861, and was readmitted as a state in 1868.

Bibliography

Douglas, Marjory Stoneman. *The Everglades: River of Grass*. Sarasota, FL: Pineapple Press, 1988.

Porter, A. P. *Jump at de Sun*. Minneapolis: Lerner, 1992.

Rawlings, Marjorie Kinnan. *The Yearling*. New York: Aladdin, 1988.

_____. *Cross Creek*. New York: Simon & Schuster, 1996.

Sneve, Virginia Driving Hawk. *The Seminoles*. New York: Holiday, 1994.

Activities

Tracking Storms

The hurricane season lasts from August to October. Prepare a hurricane tracking display with the help of students. Tack a map of North America that features the Atlantic Ocean, the Gulf of Mexico, and the Caribbean Sea on a bulletin board. Let groups of students research various topics, such as what characterizes a hurricane, hurricane names for the current year, major hurricanes that have hit the United States, and warning signs, and post their findings on the board. As the hurricane season progresses, track the storms' paths on the map.

Palmettos or Pines?

Both the Tiger and Pierce families had to rely on the natural resources around them for survival. They couldn't predict when a shipwreck would occur or what its cargo would be. Have pairs of students compare and contrast the natural resources of Florida and their own state by making resource maps for both states. Then ask them either to draw a picture of the Pierces' lumber-and-palmetto house and its floor plan or a house based on the resource maps for their state.

I Would Never Get Tired of This Book!

The Pierces had only two books in their home, but the books were read over and over again. Begin a discussion with students about what their favorite books or CDs are. See if they can narrow their favorites down to only two choices. Encourage them to explain their choices. Do students think they would be satisfied with their choices for long periods of time if, like the Pierces, they didn't have access to new books or CDs?

A Letter from Mars

Today, about the only unexplored territory is space. Encourage students to imagine that they are pioneers in space and to choose the planets they would like to live on. Ask them to research their new homes and to think about what living there would be like—especially lengths of days and nights, climate, resources, shelter, and food and water supplies. They can report their findings in letters to friends back on Earth.

Seminole Pioneers

The Tiger family in the play were pioneers in Florida before the Pierce family. The Seminole people settled in present-day Florida in the early 1800s. Guide students in researching the history of the Seminole people. After they present their findings, suggest that students collaborate on a pioneer play about a Seminole family leaving Georgia, settling in Florida, and/or having to move to Indian Territory in present-day Oklahoma.

A Visitor

CAST

ALTHEA DODD, Teacher and leader
   of a writing group

DANNY

MARY

SUSAN   Workshop members

FRANK

LAURA INGALLS WILDER, Author
   of the Little House series about her
   pioneer experiences. She is an elderly
   woman by this time.

Scene

1950. An after-school writing workshop near Mansfield, Missouri. The workshop members have been learning to write by keeping diaries or journals of their day-to-day experiences. ALTHEA DODD and the workshop members sit in a circle. There is one empty chair.

ALTHEA DODD: Did everyone bring their diaries today? Good. Because I have a surprise for you.

DANNY: Do we have a new member?

DODD: Yes, Danny, in a way we do. I've invited a friend of mine to come and speak to us. This is someone you know. Maybe you don't know her personally, maybe you've seen her around Mansfield. But in any case, you know her.

SUSAN: Wait a minute! The only famous person around here is Laura Ingalls Wilder—

DODD: That's right. Please welcome the author of the Little House books, Mrs. Laura Ingalls Wilder.

(LAURA INGALLS WILDER enters and sits in the empty chair. ALTHEA DODD and the workshop members clap.)

DODD: We're so honored to have you here, Laura.

WILDER: It's always my pleasure to meet young writers.

DODD: I'd like you to meet Danny, Mary, Susan, and Frank. (Each one smiles and nods as his or her name is called.)

WILDER: I'm very pleased to meet you all. I believe I know your families, at least a little. Susan, is your last name Swanson?

SUSAN: (looking surprised) Yes, it is.

WILDER: I know your grandmother. Her name is Susan, too. She was here in Mansfield when I first arrived.

SUSAN: She was? My grandmother was a pioneer?

WILDER: She certainly was. You're surprised to hear that?

SUSAN: Well, yes . . . it seems . . . well . . . so *long* ago.

WILDER: It wasn't, really. Look at me, I was a pioneer. I'm old, I admit, but not ancient. Things change very fast. Maybe it doesn't seem that way to you now, but when you're my age, you'll look back on today the same way I look back on the pioneer days.

DODD: And that's a good reason to keep diaries, don't you think?

WILDER: Yes, indeed. Diaries record the way your lives change, and they help you remember.

FRANK: Our experiences are boring—at least, mine are.

MARY: Nothing *ever* happens here.

WILDER: How long have you been keeping your diaries?

DANNY: Since September.

WILDER: September? That's only three months. You're still young—so are your diaries. You'll have lots of experiences. Once you've had them, you'll have memories of them. Writing and remembering are a lot alike.

FRANK: What do you remember most, Mrs. Wilder?

WILDER: What do I remember most? Oh, that's easy. Moving. My family and I moved about ten times in my life. I think moving is my earliest memory. We were living in the woods of Wisconsin, and I was just a toddler, when one day Ma and Pa announced that we were moving to Kansas. I didn't even know where Kansas was. We packed up everything we could carry in the wagon and set off, Ma, Pa, and my sister Mary.

SUSAN: Don't forget Jack, the bulldog.

WILDER: So you've read my books?

DODD: We're reading them now.

WILDER: Jack was my best friend. We might have stayed in Kansas, but by mistake we'd settled on land that belonged to Osage people. The Osage were finally forced off of their land, but that happened later. Then we were the ones who had to leave. So we moved back to Wisconsin.

FRANK: Is that when you wrote *Little House in the Big Woods*?

WILDER: No, that was much later. And if I'd been keeping a diary when I was your age, the book would have been much easier to write. I remember my family when I think of those times. Family life was different then in that survival depended on everyone doing his or her part. There was a lot more work then, when you couldn't just go the

store and buy the things you needed. You had to make them. Luckily for us, Pa was a very skilled man. I helped where I could, as a little girl. Mary and I churned butter, sewed quilts, washed dishes, and swept the floor. But my main job was to keep the fire going. In winter, if the fire went out, we could freeze before we got it going again.

MARY: Was that where you heard the wolves howling at night?

WILDER: Oh yes, the wolves. Pa was different from most pioneers in his outlook. Most just exterminated the wolves and other predators. Pa thought that living with animals was part of the point of living in the woods. That's one of the things I miss—there aren't nearly as many animals today.

FRANK: Didn't your dad like people?

WILDER: You mean because we moved when settlers came?

FRANK: I didn't mean that to insult him.

WILDER: That's all right. Pa loved that way of life. Coming to a wilderness and making a home. He didn't want it to end—maybe he had a little wolf in him. The arrival of people meant it was ending. So when the settlers came, we were on the move again—to the prairies of Minnesota near a town called Walnut Grove.

SUSAN: The soddy—

WILDER: That's right. But I've seen the sod houses pioneers built out in Kansas, and some two stories and about eight rooms. Not ours. Ours was just a dugout in the side of a streambed—

FRANK: Like a wolf's den.

WILDER: A lot like that. If you want to be close to nature, try living in a dugout. But it was just temporary because, unlike on the plains farther west, we had trees to build a real house. Pa built us a house out of sawn lumber. There's a big difference living in a log cabin than in a house made from lumber. Pa planted a beautiful wheat field, but— maybe you remember what happened to it.

FRANK: The grasshoppers ate it.

WILDER: They surely did. They wiped us out. Many other families, too. There was nothing left of that wheat but stalks when the grasshoppers got done with it. It was a plague. Do you know, after eating all our wheat they didn't have the decency to fly off with their full bellies? Instead, they

Read-Aloud Plays: Pioneers Scholastic Professional Books

died by the billions. My sister Mary and I couldn't even walk to school because the ground was covered with dead and dying grasshoppers.

SUSAN: Where did they come from? Why didn't they go back?

WILDER: I don't know. In nature, when something really unusual happens it's often because things are out of balance—there's too much or too little of something. Maybe they came to the plains because we were growing so much food. They devastated farms from 1874 to 1877, and then they just vanished.

MARY: Were you keeping a journal then?

WILDER: No. I wish I had been. But it was around then that I learned to love reading and writing, the way stories could transport me anywhere in the world. All our lives, Ma had read to us, and Pa was a great storyteller. But as I look back on it, my sister Mary was a big influence on my life as a writer. She went blind from rheumatic fever, as I guess you know. Pa asked me to be Mary's eyes. We were on the move again—this time to the Dakota Territory—and I narrated the trip for Mary. I learned a lot from that. One thing I learned was that details make a story come alive for the reader. Small things matter. Lives are made up of a lot of small events and a only a few big ones. And I tried to write my books that way.

DODD: While we were reading your books, we were talking about how things have changed for people since pioneer days.

WILDER: Yes, I was born in 1867, and I'm getting pretty old, but even so, a tremendous change has taken place.

DANNY: 1867, wow! That's just two years after the end of the Civil War and Abraham Lincoln's assassination.

DODD: Think of that. One lifetime, and all the inventions that have changed our lives since then.

MARY: Cars, airplanes.

SUSAN: The telephone.

FRANK: Electricity.

DANNY: The atomic bomb.

WILDER: The ice cream soda.

SUSAN: The ice cream soda?

WILDER: A brilliant invention. The ice cream soda was invented in 1874, and it certainly changed my life. But we haven't mentioned the railroad. The transcontinental railroad was completed in 1869—

DANNY: Five years after the ice cream soda.

WILDER: That's right. I was a child, but I remember how people talked about it—like it was a miracle, which in a way it was. I think you could say that the coming of the railroad ended pioneering in this country. Some people say that the United States wasn't a country until the railroad linked it.

MARY: Don't forget doctors. Medicine has changed.

FRANK: You're just saying that 'cause your dad's a doctor.

WILDER: Medicine has changed. I've been reading about those new medicines called antibiotics that kill infections. When I was a child, you could die from a cut on your finger.

DANNY: Pioneers must have been a lot tougher than us.

WILDER: Why do you think so?

DANNY: I don't know. It seems like it.

WILDER: It's true that people were more self-sufficient, but I don't know if they were tougher. A lot of people died young. Death was much more present in pioneers' lives than it is in ours.

MARY: My uncle was killed in World War Two.

WILDER: There you are. As a pioneer, I never had anything like world war to contend with. But I think day-to-day life was more dangerous. Plus, farming is a terribly difficult occupation. Are any of you farmers?

MARY: I'm a farmer. Well, my family has a farm. I'm Mary Curtis.

WILDER: Oh yes, I know your folks. Tell them I said hello.

MARY: I will. My father comes in from the fields—he grows wheat—and he's exhausted, you can tell. When my brother complains, my father says, "Just imagine what it would be like if we didn't even have a tractor, like in the old days."

WILDER: What are your chores around the farm?

MARY: I milk the cows and feed the chickens at five o'clock, before I go to school.

WILDER: Then you're a farmer. I wouldn't want to have been anything else, but I was glad to stop farming.

SUSAN: When did you stop?

WILDER: We settled here in Mansfield in 1894. We were still farming then, but gradually we hired help and took things a little easier than we'd been used to. My husband's health had been damaged by diphtheria, but he was happy tending our apple trees. He died just two years ago. Almanzo was a fine man, and he lived a good long life. He was ninety, you know.

FRANK: Then when did you become a writer? After you moved here?

WILDER: Yes, well after. I was sixty-five years old when my first book, *Little House in the Big Woods*, was published. So you see, you have a head start on me. That reminds me. The book came out in 1932. That was the middle of the Great Depression. Do you know about the Depression?

FRANK: Not really.

SUSAN: The Dust Bowl?

WILDER: Yes, that was part of it. Ask your parents. You can bet they'll remember. Do you ask your parents to tell you about their pasts, when they were about your age? No? As writers, you should. They have stories.

DODD: Excuse me, Laura, but I promised them I wouldn't let you be late.

WILDER: Is it time?

DODD: I'm afraid so.

WILDER: (standing up) I guess I'd better be going. They're dedicating the new library to me tomorrow, and we're having a rehearsal this afternoon. But I'd like to invite you to come to the dedication as my guests. I'll like seeing the writers of the future in the audience. Can you all come?

EVERYONE: Sure! Yes!

(The group members all stand, excited by the invitation. WILDER begins walking toward the door.)

WILDER: There's a little party afterward, and you can bring your families.... You know, you got me thinking. I'll just say this, then I've got to go. What books do, what stories do, is act as a sort of glue that attaches the past to the present so that both make more sense. That's what I want my books to do—show how it was to live here not so long ago, how things were different and how they're the same. Somebody,

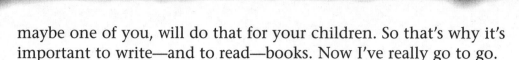

maybe one of you, will do that for your children. So that's why it's important to write—and to read—books. Now I've really go to go.

(She stops at the door.)

Yes, you all have got me thinking. They're going to ask me to say a few words tomorrow, and if you hear something along those lines, don't be too surprised. It's been a pleasure meeting you, and I'll see you tomorrow.

EVERYONE: Thank you! Bye! See you tomorrow.

DODD: The Laura Ingalls Wilder Public Library. That has a nice ring to it.

DANNY: Think they'll charge her for overdue books?

The Story Behind the Play

Laura Ingalls Wilder was born on February 7, 1867, in the big woods of Wisconsin. Laura and her family—her mother Caroline and her father Charles, her older sister Mary, younger sisters Carrie and Grace, and younger brother Charles—moved many times. They settled on the plains of Kansas, moved twice back to the big woods of Wisconsin, into a sod house in Minnesota, a town in Iowa, and a town in South Dakota. At the age of 15, Laura Ingalls began teaching school. Three years later, she married Almanzo Wilder. The Wilders moved to Missouri, where they had a daughter named Rose. Laura always told Rose stories about growing up in the big woods and on the prairie. At the suggestion of her daughter, Laura began writing down the stories. Her first book, *Little House in the Big Woods,* was a success. Laura Ingalls Wilder wrote a total of 11 books. She died in 1957 at the age of 90.

BIBLIOGRAPHY

Anderson, William. *Pioneer Girl: The Story of Laura Ingalls Wilder*. New York: HarperCollins, 1998.

Anderson, William, ed. *A Little House Sampler*. New York: HarperCollins, 1998.

Collins, Carolyn Strom, and Christina Wyss Erikkson. *The World of Little House*. New York: Scholastic, 1996.

Wade, Mary Dodson. *Homesteading on the Plains: Daily Life in the Land of Laura*. Brookfield, CT: Millbrook Press, 1997.

Wilder, Laura Ingalls. *By the Shores of Silver Lake*. New York: HarperCollins, 1987.

_____. *Farmer Boy*. New York: HarperCollins, 1987.

_____. *Little Clearing in the Woods*. New York: HarperCollins, 1998.

_____. *Little House in the Big Woods*. New York: HarperCollins, 1987.

_____. *Little House on the Prairie*. New York: HarperCollins, 1997.

_____. *Little Town on the Prairie*. New York: HarperCollins, 1987.

Activities

A Family Tree

Draw a diagram for a family tree on the board. Use your own ancestors to complete the diagram, or you may want to have students use the Little House books to help you complete the family tree for Laura Ingalls Wilder. Then tell students to see how much they can find out about the pioneers in their families. Remind them to include dates and places of births, marriages, major moves, and deaths. You may want to consult Lila Perl's book, *The Great Ancestor Hunt,* for genealogical resources. Set aside time for students to share their family trees—or, even better, invite members of their families to tell stories or show pictures and other artifacts.

This Is My Life

Laura Ingalls Wilder turned the events of her life into a best-selling series of books. Have students write and illustrate short stories about their lives. Suggest that they carry small notebooks with them during the day or write in diaries at night to record the events in their lives. Compile the stories in a binder. As the year progresses, encourage students to add more stories to the anthology. If possible, duplicate a copy of the anthology for each student at the end of the year.

When Was That Invented?

In the play, Laura Ingalls Wilder talks about the inventions that she has seen in her lifetime, such as ice cream sodas, cars, and airplanes. Have students create an invention timeline for the classroom. Brainstorm a list of everyday items that we take for granted today, such as computers, traffic signals, eyeglasses, and so on. Assign the items to different students. They should discover when the items were invented, who discovered them, and share any fascinating facts about the inventions. Make sure everyone posts his or her dates and facts on the timeline.

Twenty Questions

Who are students' favorite authors? Suggest that they write a list of questions they would like to ask the writers. Encourage students to write letters to the author containing at least one of the questions. Send letters to the authors in care of their publishing houses. You may also consider letting students use the Internet—**www.amazon.com** is an informative site—or *Something About the Author* or other library resources to see if they can find the answers to their questions.

Pioneers in All Walks of Life

Remind students that there are many different kinds of pioneers. People who are the first to do or accomplish things are often called pioneers. Challenge students to find out about pioneers in medicine, space, transportation, and other areas and present these pioneer biographies to class.

Stage Terms

blackout when the stage goes dark, usually at the end of a scene or an act

center stage the middle part of the stage

downstage the part of the stage that is closest to the audience

flashback when scenes are not presented in sequence and a scene dramatizing an earlier event is inserted into the present

offstage the part of the stage that the audience cannot see

pantomime perform without speaking

stage left the left-hand side of the stage from the actors' point of view as they face the audience

stage right the right-hand side of the stage from the actors' point of view as they face the audience

Notes